MILLENNIALS

&

MONEY

SARA MEADOWS AND WILLIAM WRIGHT

This book would not be possible if our grandparents and parents had not passed along their knowledge, life lessons, and wisdom about one of life's greatest tools: *Money*. For this reason, we dedicate this book to them: Kennith & Linda Wright, Raymond & Bettye Bennett, and Steve & Tina Wright who have taught us invaluable lessons about money. We want to continue the legacy of using our resources wisely, learning from our mistakes, and blessing others through our gifts.

CONTENTS

FOREWARD

I've been serving families in a unique vocational role for well over three decades. Fifteen years ago I began serving a group of families privately as a professional trustee. I refer to what I do now as a vocational lifestyle rather than a job. A part of my "new calling" was intended to allow me to be more available for ministry. I began to serve in a greater capacity with our student ministry at my church. Thus began my journey with the Wright children. I could tell countless stories of some hard lessons they have learned as well as tenacity and intentionality that is a driving force behind this book.

In the years that I've been honored to professionally serve families, I've seen a number of core principles lived out. Most of the families I work with have been wise stewards to the point that they would be considered wealthy. Wealth today is the goal of many and candidly an expectation of too many. I am the dad of two millennials and they are friends with Sara and Will. I see a growing wisdom and a set of financial principles being lived out by some millennials that you will read about in this book. They are the same principles that the families I serve have applied for decades and generations.

These principles are profoundly simple and universal. They are based on wisdom that stretches from the academic to the spiritual. They are covered in thick textbooks and in 2000+ verses about finances in God's word. Multiple academic majors teach core technical points that build these core principles. Sara and Will have condensed the most helpful of these core principles into this book: Millennials and Money.

Millennials are such a fun group of people to be around. They question more and then engage deeper. Millennials balance between work and play effortlessly. They desire and do community better than generations that precede them. They have a hope for the future, a willingness to learn, and they eagerly engage in social justice issues.

I believe that if we could get this simple little book into the hands of the millennial generation, our nation's economic future would be profoundly changed! Read the book!!!

Richard Newton, CTFA
Certified Trust and Financial Advisor
National Christian Foundation Senior Gift Advisor and Regional Director

ACKNOWLEDGMENTS

100% of the royalties from Millennials and Money are to be donated to Place of Hope. Place of Hope is a unique faith-based, state-licensed children's organization providing family-style foster care (emergency and long-term); family outreach and intervention; maternity care; safety for victims of domestic minor sex trafficking; transitional housing and support services; foster care recruitment and support; hope and healing opportunities for children and families who have been traumatized by abuse and neglect throughout our region. A big thank you Charles Bender, Place of Hope's Executive Director, to his long lasting commitment to our community and the children in South Florida.

CHAPTER ONE

HOW'S IT GOING?

Social media has had a tremendous impact on the way we keep in touch with the world around us. There has never been an easier way for grandparents to get a peek at what goes on in the daily lives of distant grandchildren. Additionally, friends are more "connected" than ever, constantly updating their statuses to share what they think, where they're eating, or their latest activity.

Social media provides an opportunity to instantly share with the world what is happening in our lives. As a result, it has drastically altered the ways in which others view our lives and the way we view the lives of others.

One of the primary reasons social media has changed the way in which we view the world around us, especially the view of our friends' and neighbors' lives, is that what is shared on social media often gives the false impression that everything is fine in our lives.

Many of us even unwittingly labor to produce a curated look in our portrayals of our lives on social media. Our dress needs to be impeccable, our homes perfectly decorated, and our food exquisite. Curated photos, however, do not accurately portray what is really going on in our lives, or in the lives of our friends and neighbors.

The constant barrage of curated glimpses into their lives only pressures us to conform to an impossible to reach standard, to compare favorably in our lives. Our life needs to look as perfect as our friends, as our neighbors. The high price tag of that pursuit of perfection is making unmanageable debt a very real problem for many millennials.

MIL·LEN·NIAL /mɪˈlenēəl/
"a person reaching young adulthood in the early 21st century" (Google definitions).

Whether we realize it or not, our current personal financial management has an extensive impact on our future happiness and impact on the world around us. Our finances can be a blessing or a burden. Which of those words would you use to describe your finances? How are you *really* doing in this area of your life? If your financial world isn't exactly where you want it to be, *Millennials and Money* was written for you.

Peter Thiel, the multi-billionaire founder of PayPal, was once asked what he wished he had known earlier in life. He responded, "If I could go back 20 or 25 years, I wish I would have known that there was no need to wait. …So if you're planning to do something with your life, if you have a 10-year plan of how to get there, you should ask: Why can't you do this in 6 months? Sometimes, you have to actually go through the complex, 10-year trajectory. But it's at least worth asking whether that's the story you're telling yourself, or whether that's the reality." Tim Ferris added, "What could you do in 6 months if you had a gun to your head?"[1]

Picture two scenarios. One is a debt-free version of yourself ten years in the future, able to give generously, to travel regularly, and to pursue your dreams vigorously. The second scenario is you in ten years with a mountain of debt, a constant fear of bill collectors, worried that your car will break down because you have no means of paying for repairs, stuck in an apartment you really don't like, no savings, and regularly having to borrow money from your parents to make ends meet.

---

[1]Tim Ferriss, *Tools of Titans* (Boston, MA: Houghton Mifflin Harcourt, 2016), 233.

Which scenario do you find more attractive? In order to achieve the financial goals you want to have ten years from now, *you have to start pursuing them now.*

If you dream about being debt free, you're not alone, "70% of millennials say that being debt free is a top priority for them personally."[2] USA Today recently reported that 31% of American adults are currently experiencing the joys and blessings of a debt-free reality. We wrote *Millennials and Money* to help you make this dream a reality.

COUNT THE COST:
TAKING THE ROAD LESS TRAVELED ISN'T AN EASY JOURNEY

The pursuit of a debt-free reality will not be an easy one. Some of your friends will think you've lost your mind. Here's why, it's hard to present the "perfect life" on social media when you are choosing to do without in the present in order to pursue a better life in the future.

Let's face it, thanks to the internet and social media, it has never been easier to know about all of the latest and greatest stuff that everyone "needs." Thanks to Amazon Prime and ubiquitous credit cards, it has never been easier to *buy* that stuff, either. You can have it all delivered to your door tomorrow! The various ways millennials keep up with the Joneses are now just one click away.

We can have almost anything we want immediately. Then we can tweet it, Instagram it, or Facebook it, and receive instant validation with likes, retweets, and comments about how awesome our new stuff is. That validation often fuels the impulse to repeat the process: buy more stuff I want, enjoy instant gratification, and have my friends validate my gratification. Lather. Rinse. Repeat.

---

[2]Tyler Durden, "Millennials: 70% Want to Be Debt Free, 66% Refuse to 'Gamble' In The Stock Market," *ZeroHedge* (27 Oct 2015).

Researchers have proven that social media status "likes" and positive comments release dopamine into our system similar to food, drug, sex, and adrenaline rushes.[3]

Today it is possible to download an app to solve many of our inconveniences and to reduce the "waiting time" in our lives. More people are using apps than ever before. The apps themselves are more powerful than ever before. There are even multiple apps to help us manage money and pursue a debt-free lifestyle. But there is one major problem: There is no app that can fix our unending appetite for instant gratification.

THERE IS NO APP THAT CAN FIX OUR UNENDING APPETITE FOR INSTANT GRATIFICATION.

AN INSPIRING EXAMPLE

Dick Hoyt and his son, Rick, have made headlines for disrupting the racing world. At birth, Rick was diagnosed with cerebral palsy after his umbilical cord wrapped around his neck, blocking the flow of oxygen and blood to his brain. Doctors told Rick's parents to institutionalize their son because he would never be more than a "vegetable." His parents believed, however, that given enough time they could teach him to communicate and took their son home against the doctors' instructions.

Thanks to his parents' investment, Rick not only learned to communicate by learning the alphabet and using a special computer program, he eventually graduated from Boston University.

At the age of 36, Rick asked his dad if they could run in a race together to benefit a local lacrosse player. His dad acquiesced and

[3]Susan Weinschenk Ph.D., "Why We're All Addicted to Texts, Twitter, and Google," *Psychology Today* (11 Sept 2012).

pushed his son the entire length of the five mile race in Rick's wheelchair. After the finish, Rick told his dad, "When I'm running, it feels like I'm not handicapped." Team Hoyt was born.

At that moment, Dick began training to compete in race after race with his paralyzed son. He had never raced before. Dick was training not just for himself, but to get his son through the race also. Eventually they began to complete triathlons together. Dick would use a rope around his body to pull Rick in a boat behind him as he swam the 2.4 mile first leg of the race. Then he would carry his son to the bike station, where a specialized bike with a seat on the front was waiting for them to trek the 112 mile second leg of the race. At that point he would move Rick to a custom wheelchair for the remainder of the race and push him 26.2 miles to the finish line.

Team Hoyt has now run countless marathons and countless Ironman Triathlons. Doctors told Rick's parents he wasn't worth keeping. In 2008, Rick and his father were inducted into the Ironman Hall of Fame, encouraging the world with their story.

Their accomplishment wasn't achieved by a click on a smart phone or through a downloaded app. It was the product of a decision to deal with the blood, sweat, and tears that accompany the journey down a road less traveled.

DO HARD THINGS

"Doing hard things" has become a mantra of sorts for millennials, inspiring a boom of industries, memberships, and adventures targeted at our generation. Without millennials there would be no CrossFit or Hard Exercise Works. Without millennials there would be no Tough Mudders, Spartan Races, or Rucking.

Millennials have even changed the face of the travel industry by inspiring vacations filled with rushes of adrenaline rather than rest and relaxation. Millennials spend more than $180 billion annually traveling, but the way we travel is drastically different than previous generations. 69% of millennials say they crave adventure. 78% of millennials are interested in thrilling, active vacations over lazy trips.[4] Millennials are also changing the face of business. There are currently over five million millennial millionaires and an estimated 1,810 millennial billionaires.[5] Millennials really are doing hard things.

SUMMITS ARE HARD TO REACH, BUT WORTH THE INVESTMENT

The climb to the summit of financial independence is hard and unmistakably worth it. No one climbs a mountain unless they think the struggle of ascent or the prize of finishing is worth the effort.

The moment we quit believing in the why of our journey, we will throw in the towel and quit. The pain, the effort, and the difficulty wouldn't be worth it.

You have to decide. Is debt-free living and financial independence worth the effort? We think the pain of the pursuit of debt-free living is worth it, especially when considered in light of the pain of financial bondage to spiraling credit card payments, car payments, and shrinking disposable income. The pain of saying no to simple purchases now will be much less than the pain of not being able to say yes to the pursuit of your dreams in the future.

We hope you are ready. When reading *Millennials and Money*, you will need the book in one hand, a pen in the other, and a

---

[4]Amanda, "How Millennials Travel Differently," Dangerous Business 19 June 2015.
[5]Sonal Mishra, "The millennials who made it to the Forbes list in 2016," *Forbes* (23 Sept 2016) and Robert Frank, "*How millennial millionaires made their money*," CNBC (9 June 2016).

notebook close by. Connect with us via social media and let us know you have begun to make a difference in your life. Just use the hashtag #MillennialsandMoney.

NO ONE CLIMBS A MOUNTAIN UNLESS THEY THINK THE STRUGGLE OF ASCENT OR THE PRIZE OF FINISHING IS WORTH THE EFFORT.

Let's learn together, journey together, and reach the summit together. A favorite Bible verse of ours is Ecclesiastes 4:9-12, "Two are better than one, because they have a good reward for their toil. For if they fall, one will lift up his fellow. But woe to him who is alone when he falls and has not another to lift him up! Again, if two lie together, they keep warm, but how can one keep warm alone? And though a man might prevail against one who is alone, two will withstand him—a threefold cord is not quickly broken."

Don't take the journey alone. Let's do it together!

CONNECT WITH #MILLENNIALSANDMONEY

Congratulations you've just finished Chapter 1. Before you begin Chapter 2, connect with us on social media so that we can celebrate with you and meet you personally.

CHAPTER TWO

DEBT

On April 14, 1970, Jim Lovell radioed these ominous words, "Houston, we've had a problem here," from the Apollo 13 spacecraft to the command center in Houston, Texas. Lovell and the rest of the crew knew something was wrong but not to the fullest extent of the problem.

The command center in Houston first assumed the gauges were wrong; the number two oxygen tank had exploded and critically damaged several parts of the spacecraft, leaving them with little oxygen and little power. Making matters worse, the spacecraft was more than 199,000 miles from earth. Gene Kranz, the flight director for the mission, commented,

> "Every controller stared incredulously at his display and reported new pieces to add to the puzzle. Because we thought the problems were caused by an electrical glitch, I believed we would quickly nail the problem and get back on track. It was fifteen minutes before we began to comprehend the full scope of the crisis. Once we understood the problem, we realized that there was not going to be a lunar mission. The mission had become one of survival."[6]

When it comes to finances, many millennials are doing the same thing. Tapping their knuckles on the gauges, assuming they are wrong, when, in fact, the numbers they are reporting are quite accurate. The financial issues at hand are quite severe.

---

[6]Gene Kranz, Failure Is Not an Option (New York, NY: A Berkley Book, 2001) 311.

A significant downfall of our generation is the need for instant gratification. When new phrases are added to our common vocabulary to describe shopping disorders that have popped up on the American landscape, it is safe to say, "we have a problem." Never before have medical professionals thought there was a need to discuss Compulsive Buying Disorder (CBD), Onio Mania (compulsive desire to shop), or Shopaholism.

Lorrin Koran, professor of psychiatry and behavioral sciences at Stanford University, posits that compulsive buyers are more likely to have their credit cards within $100-$500 of their credit limit and they were four times as likely to make only the minimum payments on their credit card balances than those who do not struggle in these areas. Koran also noted that the consequences for impulsive buying are significantly problematic: To name a few, these consequences have included bankruptcy, family conflict, divorce, illegal activities, and suicide attempts.[7] Our 'want-it-now' mentality is leading us to a destination from which it will be difficult to return. America quickly has become a country of spenders and creditors rather than investors and savers.

CREDIT CARDS: BLESSING OR CURSE?

Credit cards can be used wisely, but they seldom are. Stephen Pollan, popular financial author and commentator, likens credit card debt to "a plastic monkey that once attached to one's back is next to impossible to shake off."[8]

First, credit cards distance buyers from the real costs associated with products. Want proof? What did you pay per gallon of gas the last time you filled up? How much did you spend on the last head of lettuce you bought with your groceries? What is your monthly

[7]Lorrin Koran, "Compulsive Buying Disorder Affects 1 in 20 Adults, Causes Marked Distress," *Psychiatric Times* (1 Dec 2006: 1-3).
[8]Stephen Pollan, *Die Broke* (New York, NY: HarperBusiness, 1998) 34.

ESIELT

cable bill? How much did you spend the last time you grabbed a cup of coffee at Starbucks? We are not saying it is wrong to use a credit card to purchase these items. We only want to illustrate how easy it is to spend money without realizing it while using a credit card. The danger of overspending is real. Millennials may be the first generation that never knows the actual costs of the products we use every day.

Unfortunately the overspending with credit cards, quickly compounds itself in multiple areas. Blake Ellis notes that almost half of millennials are so overwhelmed by their debt that "47% said they spend over half their monthly paychecks on paying off their debts." [9]

When we are oblivious to what we are spending, we unwittingly take a ride on the never-ending merry go round of impulse buying. One could easily imagine a future Saturday Night Live skit featuring millennials playing Price is Right, guessing aimlessly at the price of various household items.

IMPULSE BUYING IS A SLOW WORKING POISON

Impulse buying with credit cards isn't immediately painful, but it will eventually catch up with you and the pain will be significant.

Think of the approach of many in our generation. If you can't pay all of your bills at the end of the month, don't sweat it, just pay the *minimum*. Our dear friends Mr. Visa and Mrs. MasterCard are here to help. They are more than willing to help us get through the month, to make life more convenient, and to deliver on our every indulgence. Need to raise your credit limit? That isn't a problem at all. Just call customer service. They are conveniently open 24 hours

[9]Blake Ellis, "Millennials 'Overwhelmed' by Debt," *CNN Money* (11 June 2014).

a day and they can raise your credit limit immediately, postponing the pain of having to say no to something you want now.

The pain isn't gone forever, though. Increased credit limits usually means spending more money that we don't have. That bill will come due, with interest compounding on your unpaid balances every month. In effect, you'll probably pay several thousands of dollars in interest by the end of the year without actually paying for the product you convinced yourself you needed immediately.

Do not fall into the trap of thinking minimum payments are "OK." Pay off as much as you can every month! In fact, if you do use credit cards you should be able to pay the total balance due each month.

DO NOT FALL INTO THE TRAP OF THINKING MINIMUM PAYMENTS ARE "OK."

Today, the average American retires with a net worth of $45,447, excluding home equity.[10] It is easy to understand how this happens when one makes 3%-7% on investments while paying 15%-23% for credit card debts. Tracy Porpora notes, "42% of Millennials say that debt is their biggest concern. This age group contributes 16% to credit cards, 15% to mortgage loans, 12% to student loans, 9% to auto debt, and 5% to medical bills."[11] No smart phone or app will ever be powerful enough to overcome the ominous power of compound interest that works *against* the borrower.

---

[10]Amelia Josephson, "Average Retirement Savings: Are You Normal?" *Smart Asset* (28 Feb 2017).
[11]Tracy Porpora, "Millennials: A Generation Drowning in Debt," *Slive* (22 June 2014).

COMPOUND INTEREST: A BLESSING OR A CURSE?

"Pay now, play later or play now, pay later." This is a quote we've heard our dad say multiple times. There is a good reason this saying has become so common: it's true. The meaning is simple. If you make large purchases with credit in your early years, you will spend years of your later life trying to pay those purchases off. On the other hand, if you can practice self-discipline and begin saving while you are young; your later years will be much more enjoyable. With wise planning, you can look forward to these big purchases instead of regretting them in the future because of the debt you have accumulated.

One of our grandfathers (affectionately known by his grandkids as "Chief") retired at the ripe old age of 43. He shared an analogy to help us understand the secret of his success. Imagine you are standing on the peak of a mountain, called Mount Compound Interest, with instructions to roll a snowball down either the left or right side. The left represents debt: compound interest working *against* you. The right represents your savings and investments: compound interest working *for* you. Whichever side you choose, the snowball will roll down hill, accumulate massive amounts of snow, and will not stop. Growing larger by the minute on its journey.

Compound interest does not take holidays, vacation days, or sick days off from work. It works around the clock 365 days a year. Simply put, thanks to compound interest, either your debt or your savings are constantly growing. It is a very liberating reality to know that it is your savings that are growing at a compounded rate instead of your debts.

CHATS WITH CHIEF: MASTERING THE BASICS

When it comes to making big purchases timing is everything. Our grandfather taught us that if you wait a few days before purchasing that item you want, you'll have time to shop for a better deal and you will have time to think about whether or not you really want that item. Chief taught us to sleep on a decision before making big purchases. If you still have to have it and you have considered the true cost of the item, then you can buy it.

Debt is not your friend. Impulse buying, by definition, is buying anything that you did not plan to purchase. The habit of impulse buying has three root causes: status, convenience, and indulgence. Our desire leads us to buy something if we want to impress someone, to buy something if it is convenient and we don't want to wait, or to buy something if we feel like we deserve it. The impulse buyer never stops to ask if it is a good idea to make a purchase. He or she never contemplates just how much will be spent on an item by the time compound interest is factored into the equation. The impulse buyer just buys what they want and doesn't consider the consequences.

Some may say our grandfather is a bit old school in his approach to financial management. However, if a guy can retire at age 43, we think those old school practices are worthy of investigation.

In addition to sleeping on big purchases, Chief encouraged us to save cash before buying. This practice helps us avoid debt we cannot afford and gives us time to make a rational, as opposed to an impulse, decision. As we have tried to implement our grandfather's lessons to purchasing and saving, we have seen the biblical wisdom approach to money.

Although Scripture does not prohibit borrowing, many have noted that there are no positive references to borrowing money in the Bible. As Proverbs 22:7 teaches us, "The rich rules over the poor, and the borrower is the slave of the lender."

LIVING DEBT FREE IS POSSIBLE

Believe it or not, becoming 100% debt free is a realistic goal for all of us. You can become debt free but it will take some work. There are millions of Americans who do not owe a single penny to anyone. They have no car payments, no house payments, no credit card payments, and no college loans. They are 100% debt free. You can be in the same position.

Many people who learn the principles to becoming debt free fail to actually follow through on the steps. They are just so much *work*! As a result, instead of seeing the light of freedom at the end of a dark tunnel, they almost perceive that light as a freight train coming to toward them. Don't fall into that trap. You *can* follow this plan and become debt free. If you are worried about your resolve to do the hard work of getting out of debt, why not make a contract with yourself to do it? Sign our contract on page 16.

I'M ALREADY IN DEBT. WHERE DO I START?

So you are already in debt, what now? Imagine taking a trip without your known origin or destination. There is a chance it will be a fruitful trip, but chances are high that you will waste time and resources. You'll take a trip, but it won't be a great trip.

CONTRACT
FORM OF COMMITMENT

I, _____, recognize that I have debt that will
PRINT YOUR NAME
not go away on its own. This contract acts as a commitment to
myself as I start to eliminate my debt. Starting today, I will be more
financially conscious and develop a plan to be a better steward
with my resources. Debt can be overwhelming but I agree to hold
myself accountable and to work diligently to eliminate it.

Sign below to affirm your commitment to becoming debt free.

I, _____, will become debt free.
PRINT YOUR NAME

_____   _____
SIGNATURE   DATE

Details matter when we take a trip. Consider the airline industry. If you go to any airline to book a flight they will request five bits of information: the number of passengers, the city of origin, the final destination, the date of departure, and the date of return.

For your trip to financial freedom, how many people are going (are you single, married, or have children)? What is your city of origin (current financial situation)? Where is your final destination (completely debt free including mortgage or free of consumer debt excluding mortgage)? When is your date of departure (when would you like to begin this journey)? When is your date of return (when do you want to reach your goal)?

Complete the chart titled, "My Trip to Financial Freedom."

MY TRIP TO FINANCIAL FREEDOM

START DATE	END DATE	MARITAL STATUS

CURRENT FINANCIAL SITUATION	END GOAL

STEP ONE - START WHERE YOU ARE

Grab your pen and paper and pull up your latest bank/financial statements.

Where is your money going each month? Your bank accounts are like financial journals. If someone read these journals, what would your life story be? What words would they use to describe you--organized or haphazard, giver or greedy, resourceful or wasteful, living on the edge or planning ahead? The management of our resources indicate our priorities. You most likely know the amounts of your "big" bills-rent, car payment, loan payments: however, if you add up the amounts of food, entertainment, and miscellaneous purchases you may be shocked. Most people who do not track closely their expenditures, ask monthly, "Where is my money going?" It is as if someone else is managing our money because we really don't know where our money is going.

Now make a list of every debt you have. This exercise can be sobering if you have never considered all of your debts before. Once you list your debts on a single sheet, it might be easy to create an electronic spreadsheet for further tracking. Once entered, sort your balances from smallest to largest. Once sorted, highlight the smallest outstanding balance you have. Set your sights on it. We'll come back to it shortly.

STEP TWO - ESTABLISH A MONTHLY BUDGET

Before you can get out of debt, you have to know how much money is coming in and where it is going. Only then can you allocate extra money toward paying off your debt. You have to know your starting point before you can embark on a journey. We'll explain how to build your budget in more detail in chapter five.

STEP THREE - TRIM NON-FIXED EXPENSES

As you begin tracking every single expenditure, you will be able to separate and prioritize expenses. Eating out, buying coffee, cable, online memberships, dry cleaning, subscriptions, club memberships, cellular data plans, and entertainment are all examples of non-fixed, or variable, expenses. Determine which of these expenses you can live without and consider dropping some of them. What is more important? An afternoon latte or taking a step toward financial freedom and independence?

You will never reach your goal of being debt free until you reign in excess spending. Cutting back on things like cable, coffee, and eating out (or whatever else you discover as non-essential and excess expenditures) will free significant cash to reduce and eventually eliminate debt.

Consider this reality: on average, you can save 10%-30% per year in interest on any portion of a credit balance you pay off early. That 10%-30% could be going into your retirement account. Then, compound interest would be working *for* you instead of against you.

STEP FOUR - ELIMINATE THE SMALLEST DEBT FIRST

Return to your list of debts. Find the smallest debt you highlighted earlier. Set your sights on paying it off. As young children, we've all had the simple satisfaction of pushing over that first small domino into a long line of dominoes and starting a chain reaction.

Imagine that satisfaction multiplied several times over as you push over your first debt balance on your way to a debt free life. That is the Domino Effect (Debt Eliminator). Once that first debt is fully paid off, the amount you were paying towards it will now be added to the amount you were paying for the second smallest amount, continuing the process until every domino, or debt, has fallen. Once you target your smallest debt to begin paying off, don't cheat.

Luis Von Ahni, a professor at Carnegie Mellon University, wanted to find out which of his students were cheating on their assignments, so he created a word and an assignment: GIRACRISTO'S Puzzle. Before class ever started, he made sure the word was completely fabricated. He then created a website with the right solution to the homework puzzle along with a system in place to track every IP address that visited the page. 40 of his 200 students visited that site looking to "google" the answer.

This assignment was always the first or second issued during a semester, and no student ever knew how he could track their cheating. "At the end of class," he would address the class, "if you come up after class and confess exactly what you did. I'll only give you a zero on this assignment."[12] If you play with fire, you're likely to get burned. You may think you can cheat with VISA, MasterCard, or other credit card companies, but the truth is you can't. Pay that debt off or the dominoes will not fall.

The Smiths are an example of how the Debt Eliminator program works. They were targeted to be out of debt in 20 years, or 240 months. By following the Debt Eliminator plan, on page 21, their debt could be paid off in the month 119 by making extra payments.

Debt elimination is a mental game as much as it is a financial game. You need to build financial confidence in yourself. Once you get that first debt paid off, you will feel victorious, slowly removing the debt shackles that are anchoring you down. The Law of Inertia is simple: an object remains in its existing state until an external force changes that state. Nothing will change your debt problem until you decide to do something about it.

---

[12]Tim Ferriss, *Tools of Titans* (Boston: Houghton Mifflin Harcourt, 2016), 332.

DEBT ELIMINATOR

THE SMITHS' DEBT BALANCES TOTAL DEBT: $198,770

Visa	$ 3,438	Student Loan	$ 13,388	Van Loan	$ 20,026
MasterCard	$ 5,512	Car Loan	$ 14,768	Mortgage	$141,638

VISA		STUDENT LOAN		CAR		VAN		MORTGAGE			
1	$3,438	1	$13,388	1	$14,768	1	$20,026	1	$141,638	61	$108,743
2	$3,072	2	$13,276	2	$14,506	2	$19,552	2	$141,532	62	$107,043
3	$2,703	3	$13,163	3	$14,244	3	$19,078	3	$141,427	63	$105,338
4	$2,330	4	$13,049	4	$13,982	4	$18,604	4	$141,321	64	$103,628
5	$1,933	5	$12,935	5	$13,719	5	$18,130	5	$141,214	65	$101,911
6	$1,573	6	$12,820	6	$13,457	6	$17,656	6	$141,107	66	$100,188
7	$1,189	7	$12,704	7	$13,194	7	$17,182	7	$141,000	67	$98,460
8	$801	8	$12,588	8	$12,931	8	$16,708	8	$140,892	68	$96,726
9	$409	9	$12,471	9	$12,667	9	$16,234	9	$140,784	69	$94,986
10	$13	10	$12,354	10	$12,404	10	$15,760	10	$140,676	70	$93,240
11	**-$387**	11	$12,235	11	$12,140	11	$15,286	11	$140,567	71	$91,488
		12	$12,117	12	$11,876	12	$14,812	12	$140,458	72	$89,730
MASTERCARD		13	$11,997	13	$11,612	13	$14,338	13	$140,349	73	$87,966
		14	$11,877	14	$11,348	14	$13,864	14	$140,239	74	$86,196
1	$5,512	15	$11,757	15	$11,083	15	$13,390	15	$140,129	75	$84,420
2	$5,444	16	$11,635	16	$10,819	16	$12,916	16	$140,018	76	$82,638
3	$5,376	17	$11,513	17	$10,554	17	$12,442	17	$139,907	77	$80,850
4	$5,307	18	$11,391	18	$10,289	18	$11,968	18	$139,796	78	$79,056
5	$5,236	19	$11,268	19	$10,023	19	$11,494	19	$139,684	79	$77,256
6	$5,165	20	$11,144	20	$9,758	20	$11,020	20	$139,572	80	$75,449
7	$5,092	21	$11,019	21	$9,492	21	$10,546	21	$139,460	81	$73,637
8	$5,019	22	$10,344	22	$9,226	22	$10,072	22	$139,347	82	$71,818
9	$4,944	23	$9,665	23	$8,960	23	$9,598	23	$139,234	83	$69,993
10	$4,870	24	$8,982	24	$8,694	24	$9,124	24	$139,120	84	$68,162
11	$4,791	25	$8,296	25	$8,428	25	$8,650	25	$139,006	85	$66,325
12	$4,313	26	$7,606	26	$8,161	26	$8,176	26	$138,892	86	$64,482
13	$3,828	27	$6,912	27	$7,894	27	$7,702	27	$138,777	87	$62,632
14	$3,335	28	$6,214	28	$7,627	28	$7,228	28	$138,662	88	$60,776
15	$2,835	29	$5,513	29	$7,360	29	$6,754	29	$138,546	89	$58,913
16	$2,328	30	$4,808	30	$7,092	30	$6,280	30	$138,430	90	$57,045
17	$1,813	31	$4,099	31	$6,825	31	$5,806	31	$138,314	91	$55,170
18	$1,290	32	$3,386	32	$6,557	32	$5,332	32	$138,197	92	$53,288
19	$759	33	$2,669	33	$6,289	33	$4,858	33	$138,080	93	$51,400
20	$220	34	$1,949	34	$6,020	34	$4,384	34	$137,963	94	$49,506
21	**-$326**	35	$1,224	35	$5,752	35	$3,910	35	$137,845	95	$47,605
		36	$496	36	$5,483	36	$3,436	36	$137,726	96	$45,698
		37	**-$236**	37	$5,214	37	$2,962	37	$137,608	97	$43,785
				38	$4,210	38	$2,488	38	$137,488	98	$41,865
				39	$3,205	39	$2,014	39	$137,369	99	$39,938
				40	$2,200	40	$1,540	40	$137,249	100	$38,005
				41	$1,193	41	$1,066	41	$137,129	101	$36,065
				42	$186	42	$592	42	$137,008	102	$34,119
				43	**-$822**	43	$118	43	$136,887	103	$32,166
						44	**-$1,364**	44	$136,765	104	$30,206
								45	$135,161	105	$28,240
								46	$133,552	106	$26,267
								47	$131,937	107	$24,287
								48	$130,316	108	$22,300
								49	$128,690	109	$20,307
								50	$127,059	110	$18,307
								51	$125,422	111	$16,301
								52	$123,779	112	$14,287
								53	$122,131	113	$12,267
								54	$120,477	114	$10,239
								55	$118,818	115	$8,205
								56	$117,153	116	$6,164
								57	$115,482	117	$4,116
								58	$113,806	118	$2,061
								59	$112,124	**119**	**-$1**
								60	$110,436		

The Smiths were making minimum payments on each debt. They were able to cut their expenses to allow them to make a $300 payment toward their Visa debt for 10 months. On the 11th month, the Smiths will add $300 to their MasterCard minumum payment. This will expedite paying off this debt. They will continue to pay off one debt at a time adding the growing payment to the next debt to eliminate quicker.

STEP FIVE - CELEBRATE YOUR VICTORIES!

Once you've successfully eliminated your smallest debt, you should celebrate. You are one step closer to being debt free. Just don't go into more debt to do it. Celebrate well, then move on to the next smallest debt balance. With each victory, you will be more motivated than ever before to knock out another debt. With hard work and discipline, you will be debt free and have even more reason to celebrate!

CONNECT WITH
#MILLENNIALSANDMONEY

We want to hear from you. Do you have a favorite quote or a question that you'd like to post? Remember to use #MillennialsandMoney and we will respond.

CHAPTER THREE

INVESTING

Have you ever played the game "Would You Rather?" It's quite simple. Someone gives you two scenarios, and you have to pick one over the other. Let's play a quick round. Would you rather be given $10,000 every day for a month or be given one penny with the promise that penny would double every day for a month?

If you chose the $10,000, you would have $310,000 at the end of a month. If you chose the penny that doubles, you would have $10.7 million at the end of the same period of time. That is the power of compound interest!

Did you make the right decision? It was a tricky decision, wasn't it? It's relatively easy to understand the linear growth of a large number being added to our bank account. It takes a bit of study to grasp the exponential growth possible in the scenario with the penny.

In Chapter 2 we covered a defensive strategy: reducing and eliminating debt. It was the first step in getting compound interest to start working for you, or to get the power of compound interest on your team.

Compound interest, a type of exponential growth, has been called the most powerful force in the universe. We tend to agree. You can't afford to have something as powerful as compound interest playing on the opposing team and expect to win. After we play defense and pay off our debts, we have neutralized the power of compound interest working against us. Now it is time to put it to work *for* us, to let compound interest join our team. It is time to go on the offense.

Three simple factors make up our offensive strategy. These factors are easy to understand and execute as you begin your journey to financial freedom. These steps aren't just for financial analysts, stock brokers, or Wall Street traders. They are for every single person, regardless of investment portfolio or prowess. Our offensive strategy consists of figuring out what we can do to get an early start on our retirement, taking advantage of absolutely free money, and resisting popular financial norms.

FACTOR ONE – THE EARLIER THE START, THE BIGGER THE RETURN

When a difficult journey stands before us, it is easy to think of a thousand different reasons why you *can't* make it. You cannot think that way in your pursuit of a debt free, financially stable life. While there are many different characteristics that separate the Millennial, Boomer, Gen Xer, they have all struggled with debt at some level.

In spite of that struggle, however, there have been individuals from each of those generations who have refused to label themselves as powerless financial victims and have made money work for them. Many millennials have joined the ranks of the bold and brave and are beginning to invest early. One study found that 74% of millennials as a generation have started saving at the young age of 22. This is 5 years earlier than Gen X'ers and 13 years sooner than Baby Boomers.[13]

We remember the first time our dad showed us this compound interest chart and talked to us about investing for retirement. Like most teenagers, we struggled to comprehend the idea of retirement because it was so far away.

This chart was a motivator, though. We didn't fully understand the chart at first glance, but we were eager to reap the benefits it highlighted. The mystery behind this chart is compound interest.

---

[13]Alicia Adamczyk, "Millennials Save For Retirement Earlier Than Baby Boomers, Survey Finds," *Forbes* (17 July 2014).

COMPOUND INTEREST CHART

	MR. WISE			MR. PROCRASTINATION	
Age	Contribution	Balance	Age	Contribution	Balance
22	$5,000.00	$5,400.00	22	$0	$0.00
23	$5,000.00	$11,232.00	23	$0	$0.00
24	$5,000.00	$17,530.56	24	$0	$0.00
25	$5,000.00	$24,333.00	25	$0	$0.00
26	$5,000.00	$31,679.65	26	$0	$0.00
27	$5,000.00	$39,614.02	27	$0	$0.00
28	$5,000.00	$48,183.14	28	$0	$0.00
29	$5,000.00	$57,437.79	29	$0	$0.00
30	$5,000.00	$67,432.81	30	$0	$0.00
31	$5,000.00	$78,227.44	31	$0	$0.00
32	$0	$84,485.63	32	$5,000.00	$5,400.00
33	$0	$91,244.48	33	$5,000.00	$11,232.00
34	$0	$98,544.04	34	$5,000.00	$17,530.56
35	$0	$106,427.56	35	$5,000.00	$24,333.00
36	$0	$114,941.77	36	$5,000.00	$31,679.65
37	$0	$124,137.11	37	$5,000.00	$39,614.02
38	$0	$134,068.08	38	$5,000.00	$48,183.14
39	$0	$144,793.53	39	$5,000.00	$57,437.79
40	$0	$156,377.01	40	$5,000.00	$67,432.81
41	$0	$168,887.17	41	$5,000.00	$78,227.44
42	$0	$187,798.14	42	$5,000.00	$89,885.63
43	$0	$202,821.99	43	$5,000.00	$102,476.48
44	$0	$219,047.75	44	$5,000.00	$116,074.60
45	$0	$236,571.57	45	$5,000.00	$130,760.57
46	$0	$255,497.30	46	$5,000.00	$146,621.42
47	$0	$275,937.08	47	$5,000.00	$163,751.13
48	$0	$298,012.05	48	$5,000.00	$182,251.22
49	$0	$321,853.02	49	$5,000.00	$202,231.32
50	$0	$347,601.26	50	$5,000.00	$223,809.82
51	$0	$375,409.36	51	$5,000.00	$247,114.61
52	$0	$405,442.11	52	$5,000.00	$272,283.78
53	$0	$437,877.47	53	$5,000.00	$299,466.48
54	$0	$472,907.67	54	$5,000.00	$328,823.80
55	$0	$510,740.29	55	$5,000.00	$360,529.70
56	$0	$551,599.51	56	$5,000.00	$394,772.08
57	$0	$595,727.47	57	$5,000.00	$431,753.84
58	$0	$643,385.67	58	$5,000.00	$471,694.15
59	$0	$694,856.52	59	$5,000.00	$514,829.68
60	$0	$750,445.04	60	$5,000.00	$561,416.06
61	$0	$810,480.65	61	$5,000.00	$611,729.34
62	$0	$875,319.10	62	$5,000.00	$666,067.69
63	$0	$945,344.63	63	$5,000.00	$724,753.10
64	$0	$1,020,972.20	64	$5,000.00	$788,133.35
65	$0	$1,102,649.97	65	$5,000.00	$856,584.02
66	$0	$1,190,861.97	66	$5,000.00	$930,510.74
67	$0	$1,286,130.93	67	$5,000.00	$1,010,351.60
68	$0	$1,389,021.40	68	$5,000.00	$1,096,579.73
69	**$0**	**$1,500,143.11**	**69**	**$5,000.00**	**$1,189,706.11**

Look at the numbers on the chart. At age 22, Rich Wise (Mr. Wise) invested $5,000 for 120 months into a fund that produced 8% annually. At age 31, he stopped investing and the total he invested equaled $50,000. Mr. Procrastination, on the other hand, didn't start investing until age 32. He invested in the same fund Mr. Wise did, which averaged an 8% interest rate. He invested for a total of 456 months, and his total investment equaled $190,000.

Our first inclination is to assume that since Mr. Procrastination invested a much larger amount in the fund, he would have more money by the time he retired. The inverse is actually true. Mr. Wise, because he started early, had approximately $1.5 million at retirement compared to Mr. Procrastination's $1.2 million, even though he invested only a quarter of the money Mr. Procrastination did. Just by starting early, Mr. Wise's return on investment was much larger than Mr. Procrastination's. The principle is clear. Start investing early.

Maybe you're not a teenager or a 20-something. What if you are already approaching 40 and haven't started investing? Look back at the chart. Look at Mr. Procrastination's ending nest egg. Let that sink in for a moment. For comparison purposes, we have been using his procrastination as a negative example, but he will still retire with approximately $1.2 million! That is a huge difference from today's average retiree who only has $5,000 in retirement savings.[14] Starting early means starting today. Regardless of how old you are, start saving today.

THE PRINCIPLE IS CLEAR.
START INVESTING EARLY.

[14]Monique Morissey, "The State of American Retirement," *Economic Policy Institute*, (3 Mar 2016).

FACTOR TWO - TAKE ADVANTAGE OF FREE MONEY

Receiving a raise from your employer is a wonderful thing. If your boss walked into your office next week and offered you an immediate cash raise of $5,000, would you take it? Of course you would. That is free money.

Even better than a raise in our annual salary, however, are opportunities to take advantage of compound interest. Your employer may offer you other ways for you to collect free money such as a 401(k), 403(b), or 457 plan. Each of these is the equivalent of receiving a large raise. They are called "Triple Threat" investments because you don't pay taxes on the money you contribute, you get matching funds from your employer, and your investment grows tax deferred. There is no other investment with this combination. These plans offer employer matching programs to incentivize you to invest in your own retirement. If you have a matching program offered to you, take advantage of the entire matched percentage and max it out every single month.

If your company offers a match for your retirement contributions, it is a free gift. This free gift is a **NO BRAINER**. Take advantage of it! For example, let's say you are making $75,000 a year and your company offers a 100% match on all your contributions up to 3% of your annual income per year. That means that you contribute $2,250 and your employer contributes $2,250 for a total contribution of $4,500. You immediately receive a 100% return on your money before it is even invested in your retirement account. Where else can you find an investment that will beat that?

Many companies' contributions for 401(k) plans are around a 3% match, but 6% is not uncommon. Take advantage of this free gift and don't let it get away. Every month, without fail, give the max amount your employer will match.

Under Factor One, we discussed the power of compound interest. Consider now the power of compound interest combined with free employer matching funds. Three factors are at work here: your regular savings, your employer's matching funds, and the compound interest being applied to *both*. If you fail to take advantage of matching funds, you're not only losing free money initially (from the match), but you are also losing hundreds of thousands of dollars in potential compound interest.

While the benefits of an employer match are quite exciting, there is a common mistake made by young adults when they begin to see their nest egg grow. They want to pull it out of their 401(k) early! This common mistake costs more than you can imagine. If you withdraw $50,000 from your 401(k), you actually only receive $29,000 (see the below chart). 25% of that withdrawal will go to federal taxes, 7% to state taxes, and another 10% is deducted for an early withdrawal penalty. After all is said and done, you only receive 58% of your funds. OUCH! Stick to the plan. Don't touch it until Retirement!

Before you consider cashing out your 401(k) in the future.

$50,000 EARLY WITHDRAWAL FROM A 401(K)

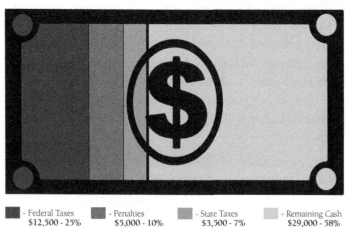

| | - Federal Taxes $12,500 - 25% | - Penalties $5,000 - 10% | - State Taxes $3,500 - 7% | - Remaining Cash $29,000 - 58% |

Why leave money on the table? Give yourself a raise. Max out your employer's match. Don't touch it and watch your money grow!

FACTOR THREE - RESIST POPULAR FINANCIAL NORMS

Recent studies show that only 24% of millennials demonstrate a basic knowledge of sound financial practices. Only 8% showed high financial literacy. If you don't know the basics, you owe it to yourself to learn.

Not only is there a lack of basic knowledge of sound financial practices among millennials, most will not seek help when they make important financial decisions. Only 27% seek professional financial advice on savings and investments and only 12%, on average, seek professional advice for debt management.[15] Millennials make up a population that will shape the future of our economy. Despite the small numbers of millennials starting to save early, the outlook for our generation still looks bleak.

When we can barely pay our bills and struggle to make ends meet, investing is rarely given a second thought. That is why it is crucial to pursue a financial strategy that will allow us to manage our budget, avoid debt, and have disposable income we can invest.

A recent survey from the American Institute of Certified Public Accountants shows that over 25% of Millennials have late payments or are dealing with bill collectors. Well over 50% are still receiving some form of financial aid from their parents.

One of the most disturbing findings of this study reveals that seven out of ten young people define financial stability as being able to pay all of their bills each month.[16]

---

[15]*Millennials at Work: Reshaping the Workplace* (PWC, 2008) .
[16]Mark Cussen, "Money Habits of The Millennials," *Investopedia* (26 July 2016).

"They don't want to ask for help, they are embarrassed,
they feel they are in this by themselves, and they are
using interesting ways, like taking cash advances on
their credit cards to try to deal with their plight."[17]

Those with higher financial literacy, tend to trust financial professionals than those whom are less financially literate.

Here are a few of the most concerning findings from a recent study of millennials and their finances by the Global Financial Literacy Excellence Center at George Washington University:

- When tested on financial concepts, only 24% demonstrated basic financial knowledge.
- Nearly 30% are overdrawn on their checking accounts.
- In the past five years, 42% used an alternative financial services product (Payday loans, pawnshops, auto title loans, tax refund advances, rent-to-own products).
- At least 54% expressed concern over their ability to repay their student loans.
- Over 20% of those who had retirement accounts took out loans or hardship withdrawals in the past year.
- Only 27% are seeking professional financial advice on saving and investing.[18]

Additionally, 4 out of 5 millennials have major debts, such as student loans.[19]

---

[17]Katie Gibson, "Degrees Don't Make Millennials Financially Literate," *CBS News* (7 Jan 2016).
[18]Ibid.
[19]Charis Brown, "Millennials' Lack of Financial Knowledge Could Be a Big Problem For The U.S. Economy," *Clark* (24 Feb 2016).

THE FIRST SCARY STEP

Remember your first bike ride, the first time you swam, or the first time you asked a girl out on a date? Each was a scary moment because it involved a risk of some kind.

On May 24, 2001, Temba Tsheri, a 16 year old, became the youngest person to climb Mt. Everest. Magnus Carlson became a chess Grandmaster at the age of 13. Pele was 17 years old when he won The World Cup with Brazil. Roger Bannister was 25 years old when he became the first person in history to run a mile in under four minutes. J. K. Rowling was 30 when she finished her first manuscript of Harry Potter. Each of these stories became a reality because each of these individuals was willing to take a scary first step. Your first scary step may be an investing class at a local school or simply asking for help from someone who knows the ins and outs of finance. Remember the three strategies we discussed above and take action. You can't afford not to!

Forget huge, gaudy financial goals for now. Take baby steps for small, daily wins. Your first scary step might be connected to investment IQ or literacy. Whatever your first scary step is be sure to share it with us on social media.

CONNECT WITH
#MILLENNIALSANDMONEY

Look back through chapter 3. What is the primary lesson learned that you will take action on in the next five days. Accountability is a powerful force. Share with us a brief action point on social media.

CHAPTER FOUR

BUYING A HOUSE

You're finally dating the man or woman of your dreams. You are each infatuated with the other and before you know it, you find yourself at the altar of a church. Congratulations, you are married! Next is the honeymoon. Off to the Caribbean. Seven days and nights in paradise and as fast as it came, it comes to an end. It's time for work, bills, and getting back to the rigors of life. Inspired by Chip and Joanna Gaines from HGTV's show Fixer Upper, you are ready to find your dream home. It is time to call your realtor to start the hunt. Adding to the pressure to buy is the fact that your lifelong friends just bought a home. You don't want to be left behind. Renting isn't as cool as owning a home. You and your spouse wonder together, "How much home can we afford? How much could we borrow?" These questions seem innocent enough and look like great places to start the process of becoming a home owner. So off you go to speak with a banker or a mortgage broker.

After looking at 8-10 homes you see the home of your dreams: freshly painted white picket fence, enclosed two-car garage, highest school zone ratings, and carefully manicured lawn. This house really is your dream home, at least for now. Before signing all the papers for a thirty-year mortgage you and your spouse have a brief discussion, "Is it really a good idea to borrow the max amount of money we can based on both of our salaries?" Then you console one another, "What could go wrong? This really is our dream house."

Unfortunately, making extra payments and paying off your mortgage early really won't be an option. You have left yourself with no expendable income. What if something bad happens? Consider just a few of the possibilities: Conflict at work could result in a demotion or layoff, one of you could have an accident, a recession could hit. What if something good happens? You discover you are expecting a baby.

It pays to step back from a major purchase and consider all of the possibilities. The Bible teaches us that "The plans of the diligent lead surely to advantage, but everyone who is hasty comes surely to poverty" (Proverbs 21:5).

For most Americans the purchase of their home is the single largest investment they will make in their lifetime. Unfortunately, according to Zillow, Americans are buying increasingly expensive first homes and spending more of their relative incomes than any time in the past 40 years.[20] They are house poor.

We are going to show you in this chapter exactly why it is a bad idea to follow this current trend. While homeownership is certainly recommended, how someone purchases that home is vitally important. Since the early 70s, the average age of a first time homeowner has remained relatively unchanged (30.6 years compared to 32.5 today). A shocking difference, however, is the price of that first home to income ratio, which has climbed during the same time period from 1.7 to 2.6.

Basically, that means that if the average income in an area is $100,000, the average price of a home would be $260,000. In some parts of the US this ratio is higher and in others it may be lower. We will see in this chapter why a lower purchase price to income ratio is essential for millennials who desire to live debt free.

---

[20]"Today's First Time Homebuyers Older, More Single," *Zillow* (17 Aug 2015).

"THE PLANS OF THE DILIGENT LEAD SURELY TO ADVANTAGE, BUT EVERYONE WHO IS HASTY COMES SURELY TO POVERTY." -PROVERBS 21:5

THE POWER OF EXPECTATIONS

Few research projects have garnered as much attention and controversy among educators, researchers, and the general public as Rosenthal and Jacobson's Pygmalion Study. For the study, middle school students in San Francisco and college students in Portland, Oregon were observed. In the study, teachers were given two randomly divided classes. The teachers were then told that one class was made up of the "best and brightest students" and the other class was made up of "slower, average students." Although the students in each class were statistically the same prior to separation, the outcomes of the classes varied quite differently. The students from both states in the "best and brightest" class rose to meet the expectations their teachers had for them. The classes where the teachers were told the students were "slow and average" fell behind expected benchmarks.

When a student in the "bright" class couldn't answer a question the teacher reasoned that they must simply be having a bad day. When a student in the "average" class didn't know the answer the teacher often reasoned that these students would never understand the issue because they were too "slow." Even though these students were exactly the same academically, their results varied drastically entirely based upon their teacher's expectations of them. Expectations are very powerful. Expectations function like a rudder on a ship. Though small in size compared to a ship, the rudder sets the ship's trajectory.

Speaking of the power of expectation, Henry Ford once said, "Whether we think we can or whether we think we can't, we are right."

We all have financial expectations. Some believe they will always struggle financially. Others might lament that, "No matter how hard I try, I will never get ahead." Unfortunately, those expectations often become self-fulfilling prophesies. Our mindset has to change and we have to set realistic expectations. Instead of purchasing our dream home first, millenials have to realize that buying a home they can actually afford will set them up for financial freedom in the future. Knowing what fits in your housing budget, not just what the bank tells you that you can afford, is the most crucial part of buying a house. To do this, you first have to understand how mortgages work and why you need to buy your second home first.

"WHETHER WE THINK WE CAN OR WHETHER WE THINK WE CAN'T, WE ARE RIGHT."

UNDERSTAND HOW MORTGAGES WORK

Step one of buying a home is understanding what a mortgage is. First, start with the word "mortgage" itself. The word mortgage is made up of two Latin words, "mortuus" and "gage". "Mortuus" means death and "gage" means to pledge. According to John Ayto's Dictionary of Word Origins, "The notion behind the word is supposedly that if the mortgagor fails to repay the loan, the property pledged as security is lost, or becomes 'dead,' to him or her." To this very day if the debtor does not pay the lender, the house and property are returned to the one who holds the mortgage.

Mortgage is broken up into two parts: a principal payment and interest payment. The principal payment is the money used to pay down the balance of the loan, while the interest is paying the bank for use of their money. When you buy a home, an amortization schedule will be given to you by your lender. This schedule will show you how your monthly payments will be divided between principal and interest. In a typical 30 year mortgage, your monthly payment will be comprised mostly of interest for the first fifteen years. Understanding how much interest you are paying over the course of your 30 year loan should motivate you to make extra payments above the minimum amount. This will allow you to pay off your home much sooner than 30 years and save thousands in interest!

BUY YOUR SECOND HOME FIRST

Out of fear, many millennials are avoiding homeownership altogether and as a generation are being labeled "lifelong renters."

Millennials have a host of reasons for not buying or postponing homeownership: insufficient credit scores, no down payment, inability to pay the closing costs, insufficient income for monthly payments, and too much existing debt. Millennials want to purchase a home and build equity, but the prospects of homeownership become more elusive with each passing day.

The fears associated with homeownership are real, but fear isn't all bad. Fear is the beginning of wisdom. Proverbs 9:10 says, "The fear of the LORD is the beginning of wisdom, and the knowledge of the Holy One is insight." Often it is our fears that allow us to examine, research and learn from others. Typical second home purchases (investment properties) are made with the following priorities: location, home costs, and a healthy emotional detachment. A second homebuyer might want a mountain home near the Smoky Mountains, a beach they like to frequent, or extended family. In each of these examples, location is paramount. Because a second home will only be visited periodically, a smaller house is sufficient.

A smaller home usually means a smaller price for the home. It also means lowered insurance cost, electricity bills, and upkeep. Since the second home is simply an investment, the buyer is more emotionally detached. Typically second homeowners aren't buying expensive upgrades or top of the line furniture. They are also usually willing to let a few things go until they need to put the house back on the market as an investment to sell or rent.

By entering the home buying process with the priorities of someone buying a second home (location, low cost, healthy, emotional detachment) you provide yourself with a distinct purchasing advantage. When millennials buy their second home first, location will be central to their purchasing strategy. Location savvy purchasers carefully consider proximity to the highest rated schools, recreation, healthcare and entertainment. Where are the city commissioners expecting growth over the next ten years? Where are the next proposed trash incinerators being built?

Just as important is the priority of home costs. If your mortgage agent tells you that they will loan you $200,000, buy a home that costs $160,000. If you can borrow $500,000, buy a $400,000 home. Remember that you are buying your second home first and that this first home is an investment foundation that you will build a life upon. Buy your first home for 80% of what the bank will loan you (at most).

Now you are prepared to make extra payments on your mortgage, pay off you school loans, automobiles, credit cards, and other debts upon which you are accumulating interest. In the end you will still purchase a suitable home and have it completely paid for in a fraction of time. You will also realize the benefits of reduced insurance, power bills, upkeep, and much more.

A dream home is a home that is paid for in full, not a house payment that gives you ulcers and keeps you on the wrong side of the interest snowball. A healthy emotional detachment prevents you from meshing your personal identity with your home. You are not your home and your home is not you. A healthy personal detachment will allow you to see your house exactly for what it is, an investment. Seeing your house as an investment gives you the peace of mind of knowing your slightly smaller house gives you a distinct advantage toward building wealth and maximizing generosity.

RENTING ISN'T ALWAYS BAD

Homeownership isn't a wise move for everyone. In fact, there are many valid arguments for renting. Cost burdens associated with housing are a big issue today. Renting should remain a viable option especially for first time homebuyers. This is why online "rent vs. buy" calculators are so helpful.

When deciding whether to rent or buy here are a few helpful tips:

- Use an online "rent vs buying" calculator
- How much can you put towards a down payment?
- Consider other costs associated with homeownership (lawn maintenance, roofing, a/c, heating, electrical)
- How long do you plan to live in the area?

Financial literacy, buying your second home first, and trimming home costs are the three simple steps that lay an incredible foundation for growing your net worth. Reducing debt, effective budgeting, investing, and accumulating wealth become nearly impossible when the primary portion of your income is stretched as far as it will go every month.

CONNECT WITH
#MILLENNIALSANDMONEY

What are some characteristics you want to find in your second house? After reading about buying your second home first, share with us what you find is most important in that decision!

CHAPTER FIVE

BUDGETING

Let's be honest. No one really likes to budget. We have to admit that it isn't the first thing that comes to mind every morning. If you are anything like us, you don't like to budget, you like to spend.

As we began writing this chapter, our mind easily ran to all the things we currently "needed" to purchase. Unfortunately, EVERYTHING we were currently thinking of are liabilities.

Liabilities are all the things that take money away from us: cars, trips, clothes, surfboards, archery and fishing equipment, etc. Liabilities not only take money away from us, they also depreciate very quickly. A car is a great example of a liability. You buy it brand new and the second you drive it off the lot it is worth substantially less. The average midsize sedan depreciates $7,200 the first year of ownership.

An asset, however, is something we purchase that brings us passive income and appreciates in value. A budget helps us track, trim, and target our liabilities and assets.

A BUDGET HELPS US TRACK, TRIM, AND TARGET OUR LIABILITIES AND ASSETS.

WHO SHOULD HAVE A BUDGET?

A budget is much like the dashboard of our car. If we ignore the speedometer too long, we may soon see red and blue flashing lights in our rear view mirror. A pricey speeding ticket is likely to follow. If we ignore the gas gauge for too long, we can find ourselves stranded on the side of the road. If we ignore the odometer and oil gauge too long, the likely consequence will be a trip to the mechanic for an expensive new motor.

Whether we acknowledge the gauges or pretend they aren't there, the benefits and consequences of what they report remain consistent. The same is true with a budget. Whether we admit it or not, we all have a budget. For those who aren't paying attention, built in measures are there to remind us of our budget: bank overdrafts, credit card late fees and higher interest rates, evictions, foreclosures and bankruptcy hearings.

A budget is for anyone that wants to build wealth in order to practice generosity. A budget is a spending plan that monitors the amount of money coming in and what is going out. It allows you to track, trim, and target exactly where your money is going month after month, setting you on a clear trajectory of financial freedom. Honestly, it isn't easy to track every dollar that you make and spend, but it is easier than the pain of financial bondage.

The budget you establish for yourself must have obtainable, realistic goals that you can track every month and every year. For millennials, a budget is absolutely necessary to stop the cycle of living paycheck to paycheck.

A BUDGET IS FOR ANYONE THAT WANTS TO BUILD WEALTH IN ORDER TO PRACTICE GENEROSITY.

BUDGETING

Good news! Some millennials *are* budgeters! According Maggie McGrath, "Mud-slinging old-folk might want to take note: The 18 to 34-year-old crowd is not only better about tracking their spending and sticking to a budget than Baby Boomers, but more of them have increased their 401(k) contributions in the past year, too."[21] The same T. Rowe Price study also found that Millennials are saving an average of 8% of their annual salary toward retirement. Budgets are for those who desperately want to have compound interest working in their favor.

MILLENNIALS VS. BABY BOOMERS STICKING WITH A BUDGET

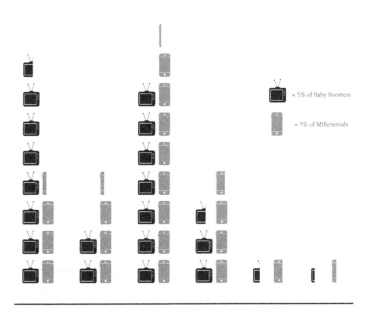

= 5% of Baby Boomers

= 5% of Millenenials

| I don't have a budget | I have a budget that I follow exactly | I have a budget that I follow most of the time | I have a budget that I follow some of the time | I have a budget, but I don't follow it | I don't know |

Source: Kelly B. Grant Aug 16 cnbc.com

BEFORE YOU START

Ultimately, it is our motives that drive us. Andy Stanley, pastor and author, wrote in his book Fields of Gold, "[God] wants you to go home, look at your bucket of seeds, and determine in your heart how much you'd like to sow. He wants you to consider thoughtfully your current circumstances, your life, your potential, and your finances. He wants you to involve your family. He wants you to pray about it. And then He wants you to come up with a plan."[22] God expects us to be good stewards of His resources so that we can give back to those in need.

We hope that your desire to give is a bigger motivation behind your budget than is your desire to accumulate things. The desire to give is stronger and more enduring. Stanley continued, "Any fear associated with giving to God's kingdom is irrational. It's on par with a farmer who, out of fear of losing his seed, refuses to plant his fields. The principle of sowing and reaping applies to our finances. Those who sow generously can expect to reap generously and receive a bountiful return."[23]

Living on a budget is the first step of looking at our bucket of seeds and determining how we might best sow (or invest). A budget first determines expenditures and then instructs how we invest and bless others. It's much more than having a bunch of numbers on a piece of paper or electronic spreadsheet.

When Jesus wanted his followers to understand the importance of finances with regard to what was happening in their hearts, he taught them "Where your treasure is there your heart will be also" (Matthew 6:21). Your heart will align with your treasure.

How we spend our money really is an outside indicator of what is happening in our hearts. Think about your budget like the plumbing in your house. You want everything coming in to be directed exactly to the right places and you also want things to leave your house through the correct channels. That only happens with our finances when we write it down and intentionally take control of our spending habits and develop a game plan (budget).

YOU CAN DO IT

Starting a budget is not a complicated process like many make it out to be. Grab a legal pad, download an app like Mint or Buxfer, or open an Excel spreadsheet. Take 20 minutes to sit down and work through these next six steps and you'll be on your way to creating a useful and sustainable budget.

1. GET PAID.

Write down your monthly income, which is the total of all paychecks received. If you are married, add your spouse's income (if any) to get a total amount.

2. LIST EVERY EXPENSE.

Write down every bit of money that is outgoing:

- **Giving** - Tithe/Contributions to your Church, Charities, Donations, Gifts
- **Housing** - Mortgage/Rent, Utilities (Electricity, Gas, Water/Sewer, Trash, Cable/Internet), Phone, Home Maintenance/Repairs, Homeowners' Insurance and Property Tax (if not included in your mortgage payment)
- **Auto** - Loan Payment, Insurance, Fuel, Repairs/Maintenance, State property tax on automobiles (if applicable)

---

[21]Maggie McGrath, "Millennials: The Money-Conscious Generation?" *Forbes* (22 June 2015).

- **Food** - Groceries
- **Insurance** - Medical, Dental, Life, Other
- **Clothing** - Clothes, Shoes, Accessories, Dry Cleaning
- **Entertainment** - Dining Out, Movies, Sporting Events, Hunting/Fishing, Country Club Memberships, Gym Memberships, Other
- **Medical** - Doctor, Dentist, Medications, Medical Supplies
- **Miscellaneous** - Toiletries, Haircuts, Incidentals, and expenses that do not fit in a category above.
- **Savings** - Contributions to Savings account, College Fund, Emergency Fund, Retirement
- **Debt Reduction** - Extra credit card payments, School Loans, other loan payments not included in categories above
- **Travel** - Airline tickets, Cruise, Rental cars, Hotel, Vacation rental homes, Tours, etc.
- **Childcare/School** - Private School, Daycare, Private Lessons, other school expenses

---

WWW.CROWN.ORG AND WWW.FINANCIALMENTOR.COM HAVE HELPFUL DEBT SNOWBALL CALCULATORS TO HELP YOU STRUCTURE AND ALLOCATE APPROPRIATE FUNDS.

---

3. FIND THE DIFFERENCE.

Subtract expenses from income. What's left? This is called your discretionary income. Discretionary income is usually the money that you don't know where it is going because you don't have a plan for it. It is used for impulse buys, vacations, luxury items, and non-essentials. This is the money that we want to put to work to help you reach your goals. If you don't have any income left after paying for the essentials like shelter, food, and clothing, then you may need to reduce expenses or increase your income.

---

[22]T Andy Stanley, Fields of Gold (Massachusetts: Tyndale, 2004), 84.
[23]Ibid., 135..

4. SET FINANCIAL GOALS.

Be specific in setting both savings and debt reduction goals. It is always easier to know if you have achieved your goals if you start with specific, realistic goals.

In Chapter 2, we discussed how to set goals for reducing your debt. In Chapter 3, we discussed the importance of starting early in contributing to your retirement fund. There is also a very important part of your budget that is essential: savings. You may have heard the saying, "I'm setting this money aside for a rainy day." This idea is to be prepared for life's inevitable unexpected expenses. These unexpected expenses can pop up in many ways such as your car breaking down, your friend asking you to be in their wedding, or you having a medical emergency.

Our dad has always taught us to "pay yourself first." What he wanted us to learn is to get into the habit of tithing and saving first, then paying your bills. He cut his grandmother's grass and when she paid him, she had three mason jars in which his wages were distributed: Church, Savings, Steve. His grandmother was wise in teaching our dad that if he didn't discipline himself to set aside money for your church and putting money into savings, then all of his money would quickly disappear. This was a simple concept that he learned, but it definitely influenced the way he and mom developed their budget from the beginning. No matter how small the amount is, you need to discipline yourself to set aside a portion of your income to put into savings.

Practically, what does a savings account consist of? Your savings account needs to consist of three parts: an emergency fund for unexpected expenses, a set aside amount for large planned expenses, and funds in case of loss of income. First, we would suggest putting up to $1,500 into your savings account for those inevitable unexpected expenses. Second, if you are planning a vacation or need to make a major purchase, then take the total amount you will need to save and divide by the months until that purchase takes place. This will give you the amount you need to set aside each month. Third, most financial advisors recommend that you have 3 months of your current income in savings just in case you lose your monthly income.

A BUDGET MAY APPEAR RESTRICTIVE, BUT IT IS ACTUALLY A STEP TOWARDS EXPERIENCING TREMENDOUS FREEDOM.

---

5. REALIGN CASH FLOWS BASED ON ESTABLISHED GOALS.

Give every dollar a job. Think about how hard you have worked and sacrificed to make every dollar you are paid. Now is the time to put every one of these "hard earned" dollars to work for you.

6. STICK TO YOUR PLAN AND STAY OUT OF DEBT.

It is *impossible* to get out of debt while simultaneously borrowing more money! You (and your spouse) have to make a decision that now is the time you are going to start living within your means. A budget allows you to do just that. A budget may appear restrictive, but it is actually a step towards experiencing tremendous freedom.

If you want something that you can't afford at present, delay the purchase until you are out of debt or until you've saved the money to purchase the item.

3 IMPORTANT POINTS ON BUDGETING

1. TRACK - LET'S SEE WHERE WE ARE.

Colossians 3:23 says, "Whatever ever you do, work heartily, as for the Lord and not for men."

Imagine the end of the NBA Finals with 5 seconds on the clock. You have time for only one more shot. Your coach calls a timeout, brings you into the huddle, and informs you that your team's success is all dependent upon you. You've made it this far and it's time to bring it home. You've never been more motivated to succeed. As you walk back onto the court, you realize the coach forgot to mention one important item: which play to run. When it comes to pursuing healthy financial management, you are the one responsible for your success. Your budget is the playbook and each expenditure provides an opportunity to call the appropriate play. Whether it's trimming your cable or afternoon latte or choosing to invest leftover money, *you make the call.*

A budget reveals if you are overspending. To determine if you are, find out how much you're spending for one category in a given year. Divide that amount by 12. If you see that it is impossible to set aside that amount per month, guess what? You are overspending. Figure a way to trim or re-prioritize that category.

Here are some good percentages to help you target where your spending should be as you develop your first budget:

BUDGET PERCENTAGE TARGET		
HOUSING - 38%	CLOTHING - 5%
AUTO - 15%	**MEDICAL/DENTAL - 5%**
FOOD - 12%	MISCELLANEOUS - 5%
INSURANCE - 5%	**SAVINGS - 5%**
ENTERTAINMENT - 5%	DEBT PAYMENTS - 5%

If you're out of these ranges, step back and look at the entire story. These categories are helpful because they set guide rails for us to gauge where we stand. If you are missing the mark, make the appropriate adjustments to align with these marks. You may have to make adjustments to the percentages if you have other categories.

2. TRIMMING - DISCIPLINE THAT GIVES DIRECTION.

Jim Rohn, a successful entrepreneur, author, and motivational speaker, once said, "We must all suffer one of two things: the pain of discipline or the pain of regret and disappointment." Living within your means is a sure way to free up cash flow to pay off debts, invest for retirement, and reach your financial goals. Just as the pain of physical training prepares us to be a better athlete, the pain of budgetary discipline will free us to reach our financial goals. Keep your eyes on the finish line and keep running. There are literally hundreds of ways to trim your expenditures.

Recently, our mom purchased a used Chevy Volt Hybrid. The cost was practically the same as the regular car she wanted, but the Volt got much better gas mileage. Now, her monthly gas bill is almost negligible. She now pays under $20.00 a month for gas. Before she bought the Volt she was driving a Suburban and spending over $200.00 each month on gas. This one decision has helped my parents save over $2,100.00 a year.

3. TARGET - DETERMINE A FINISH LINE.

You will never reach the finish line if you don't know what, or where, it is. Everyone has to know where he or she is trying to go. Your budget is important for that very reason. It lets you know how much will be left over after all of your bills are paid. Then, and only then, can you determine what to allocate to paying off debt or investing. Your budget serves as a tool that clearly outlines where money should be allocated to help you get to the finish line.

WAIT! THIS DOESN'T ADD UP.

The first time you complete your budget, it will most likely be incorrect due to one section: "Miscellaneous." Most people estimate this category because they are not tracking it. They rarely estimate accurately.

We'd venture to guess you couldn't tell us within $50 how much is in your savings account and within $100 how much you live on each month. If you don't track it, you are running in the dark. Running in the dark is not the safest way to start an exercise program.

Einstein once said, "Everything should be made as simple as possible, but not simpler." This is also true of budgets. Get all the basics down and don't leave any gaps, like vacations or clothes. If you don't know how much money you have or how much you are spending, you are likely overspending each month. In order to successfully attain your financial goals, you must reverse the process of overspending. You got into debt by overspending. You can only get out of debt by underspending.

WAYS TO BUDGET

Envelope System, Accounting sheets, or Spending Journals are all great ways to maintain a budget. Our generation has access to incredible apps and even software like Microsoft Excel that enable us to build out our own particular budget. Take advantage of these tools. Don't make the mistake of thinking you can "eyeball" it or keep track of all of your expenditures mentally. It is not possible. You will end up cheating on your budget. Get into the habit of utilizing whichever system fits your personality best.

There are several apps available that sync to your checking account and will automatically track major spending categories for you. Our favorites are Mint and Buxfer. It is still up to you to determine your fixed needs, like rent or phone bills, variable expenses, such as gas or food, and lastly wants, coffee or movies. The tighter your spending becomes on wants and variable expenses, the more you can save and invest. If you can sacrifice the time to budget, follow your budget, and stick with it for the long haul, you will have the flexibility to retire early, go on your dream vacation, or even buy that old Corvette you've been eyeing since middle school.

CONNECT WITH
#MILLENNIALSANDMONEY

Budgets, budgets, budgets... from what you learned in this chapter, connect with us and share why you think budgets are mandatory to succeeding in your journey! What is the first step you're going to take?

CHAPTER SIX

PITFALLS

We all have different motivations. Once a young man hired a dating coach because he was depressed over his inability to get a date. He had gained a lot of weight after college and lacked the confidence to ask anyone out. He told his dating coach, "I've tried everything I know to do to lose weight and nothing seems to work." His dating coach, who had helped hundreds of men get dates, was confident he could help.

The following morning the dating coach sent a beautiful young lady to the man's house dressed in her most appealing workout gear. When the man answered the door bell, she said, "If you catch me I will go on a date with you." The young man chased her all morning long, every day for six months.

Over time, the man lost 85 pounds and was getting in great shape. With each day he was closer to catching the woman of his dreams. Finally, he was convinced that the next morning would be the day he finally did. He got up early, stretched, and was at the door when he heard the knocking. When he opened the door the girl of his dreams had been replaced by a woman that was his size before he started losing weight. The young man asked if he could help the lady. She replied, "My dating coach told me to be here at 8:00 and that if I could catch you that you would date me." We all have different motivations in life. Learning what they are will help you reach your goals in life.

When it comes to finances, some are motivated by the prospect of great wealth while others are motivated by the fears of great loss. Many are motivated by the opportunity to be more generous in their lives, especially when it comes to investing in their church. The beauty of wise financial decisions is that they work regardless of your individual motivations.

Manoj Arora in *Rat Race to Financial Freedom* concluded that, "To achieve what 1% of the world's population has (financial freedom), you must be willing to do what only 1% dare to do, hard work and perseverance of highest order."

Contemporary news content is filled with stories of millennials who are achieving great success and securing financial freedom for themselves. What each one each of them has in common is that they acted on the course of direction they had made with regard to their finances. Decisions without actions accomplish nothing. To realize your dreams, you have to take action!

What are your dreams? What immediate steps are you willing to take to reach them?

LET'S TAKE A TEST

Millennials in general are well educated. We have more access to more knowledge than any generation in the history of the world. We can attend almost any university we desire thanks to the internet and online education. The wealth of the world's knowledge is literally at our fingertips. Don't know the answer? Just ask Google.

In spite of the access we have to information, however, most millennials do not pursue that information when it comes to finances. In a recent study, only 8% of millennials were able to answer the following five questions.[24] Why don't you take a stab at the questions (before you consult Google).

---

[24]Annamarie Lusardi, "The Alarming Facts About Millennials and Debt," *Wall Street Journal* (5 Oct 2015).

FINANCIAL LITERACY TEST

1) If you had $100 in a savings account and the interest rate was 2 percent per year, how much would you have in the account after five years if you left it untouched?

A. More than $102
B. Exactly $102
C. Less than $102
D. Do not know

2) Imagine that the interest rate on your savings account was 1 percent per year and inflation was 2 percent per year. After one year, would you be able to buy more than, exactly the same, or less than you could today with the money in this account?

A. More than today
B. Exactly the same as today
C. Less than today
D. Do not know

3) Is the following statement true or false? "Buying a single company stock usually provides a safer return than a stock mutual fund."

A. True
B. False
C. Do not know

4) If you had $100 in a savings account and the interest rate was 20 percent per year. After five years, how much money would you have if you never made any withdrawals from the account?

A. More than $200
B. Exactly $200
C. Less than $200
D. Do not know

5) If the interest rate falls, what should happen to bond prices?

A. Rise
B. Fall
C. Stay the same
D. Do not know

ANSWERS ON NEXT PAGE

How did you do? Don't stress if you didn't get a perfect score. If you made a perfect score, let's see how these test scores shape your everyday practice of making the most common elementary financial decisions.

The pitfalls we will discuss in this chapter can be viewed like the current in a fast moving river. It is possible to swim against the current, but it is tiring and not possible for extended periods of time. Avoiding common financial pitfalls will help you swim with the stream, which is not only easier, but will help you reach your destination more quickly.

PITFALL 1 - THE NEW CAR

Don't buy a brand new car! The moment you drive it off the lot, it instantly loses 11% of its value. If you just bought a $30,000 vehicle, that means a loss of $3,300 in the first mile of traffic. Can we ever justify buying something that loses over a tenth of its value that quickly? We have done the math. Trust us, the answer is no.

Forget about the new car smell. Use air fresheners. Make the power of depreciation work for you and not against you. By purchasing a car 1-3 years in age, you let someone else take the initial 11% depreciation hit for you. The average American will own approximately 10 cars during their lifetime. Imagine how much you would accumulate in compound interest if you invested that 11% each time you purchased a vehicle! The rate of depreciation actually decreases as the car gets older, meaning the older the car is when you buy it, the less of a hit you will take. Buying a used car is just one way to start swimming with the current financially.

Consider a few of the benefits of buying used: Lower depreciation, lower payments, less money spent on interest

Answers from Financial Literacy Test on previous page
1. A   2. C   3.B   4. A   5.A

payments, lower insurance costs, less tax paid on the initial purchase, and lower registration fees. We agree that nothing beats that "new car smell." Just remember that sweet aroma comes with a steep price tag.

Our dad drives a Chevrolet Suburban that currently has 289,000 miles on it. He and my mom bought this car used with 50,000 miles on it. When this car was nearing 100,000 miles many of his friends began to ask if he was going to trade it in before he started having to many mechanical issues. He thought about it. He had no car payment and low insurance premiums so he decided to see how many miles he could put on the vehicle before it finally died. Our dad has had *some* mechanical problems over the years. But they were cheaper than a new vehicle by far.

Car Repair Costs

New Batteries	$125
Brakes (front and rear)	$600
Tires	$700
Oil Change	$30/each
Belts	$100
Upholstery	$500

Even with these added expenses to an old, used Suburban, the "new car smell" accompanied with high dependability doesn't seem to justify itself. Avoiding the purchase of a new car does not mean you have to buy a junker. Rather, it means buying something within your means so you can avoid the accumulation of unnecessary debts. Remember your goal: financial independence.

---

[24]Annamarie Lusardi, "The Alarming Facts About Millennials and Debt," *Wall Street Journal* (5 Oct 2015).

PITFALL 2 - LEASING A CAR

The alluring appeal of leasing an automobile is an obvious one. You can drive a brand new car with extremely low monthly payments. What makes leasing attractive to the car dealership is that the lessor (you) actually pays for depreciation and interest with your monthly payments while you have the car. At the end of the lease the car dealer owns the car but you have taken the hit for depreciation, payments, and interest for the dealer. The dealer is now free to sell or lease the car a second time making another profit. It actually sounds like a great deal for everyone, initially.

When you return the leased car, however, there are usually a few extra surprises: acquisition fees, disposition fees, lease costs, excess mileage charges, and the inevitable "poor condition" fee almost everyone has to pay. It can add up to what you would have paid had you bought the car outright, only now you don't own a vehicle. Let's be smarter than the car dealership. Who really "wins" with a leased vehicle? It's not you.

If you run into financial difficulties during the lease, the car company simply repossess the automobile with a few extra costs associated. Now you owe the remaining balance, excess wear-and-tear, cost of repossession, and costs related to resale. If you owned a car instead of leasing, you could at least sell it when you encountered a financial hit.

Play long ball when it comes to your car purchase. Think of a car purchase in ten year intervals instead of jumping on the leasing treadmill of convenience. The benefit of buying is obvious. At the end of the term of your loan (which is still very close to leasing), at least you own the car. After your loan is paid, you have zero car payments, zero interest, and no mileage restrictions.

PITFALL 3 - MINIMUM CREDIT CARD PAYMENTS

If you have a $2,000 balance on a credit card with 18% annual rate and make the minimum payment of 2% of the balance (or $10, whichever is greater), it would take 370 months or just over 30 years to pay off. During that time, you would pay almost 150% more than the original price of the products you charged. Let that sink in. Imagine a lifetime of this type of financial (mal)practice. Someone getting ahead financially while making minimum credit card payments is about as easy as it would be to swim up and over the Niagara Falls (without a lifejacket). Your chances of success are pretty slim.

The credit card companies know what they're doing. They make the minimum payment look appealing. After all, the more you make the minimum payment, the more money they make. Your bill looks like this: Total Owed - $3,500, Minimum Payment - $87.50. Who wants to pay more than they *have* to pay?

While it feels GREAT to pay the minimum and hold onto that extra cash, do not be deceived! You are only hurting yourself when you make the minimum payment.

Sixty-five percent of Americans carry a balance on their credit cards. As a country, we now owe over $900 *billion* dollars in credit card debt. In spite of that unseemly number, the Nilson Report actually has great news related to Millennials and their credit card use. "It's pretty clear that young people are not interested in becoming indebted in the way that their parents are or were."[25] For all the negative press millennials receive, this news is actually good. Be forewarned, however. Credit card companies pursue their future clientele with tempting offers in an effort to get us to live with balances on our cards.

---

[25]Sarah Anderson, "Millennials Avoid Credit Cards and Their Accompanying Debt," *Deseret News* (21 Aug 2016).

They know that once this plastic monkey attaches itself to our backs, it is nearly impossible to shake. Credit card appeals to our desire for instant gratification. You can have whatever you want now. Larry Burkett and Dave Ramsey have taken hard line stances against credit card balances. Burkett often says, "If your credit card statement comes in and you can't fully pay your balance. Preheat your oven to 450 degrees and insert all of your credit cards."

Dave Ramsey coined the term "plasectomy". If you can't pay your cards off, cut them all up. Visa and Mastercard are the big ones, but even store credit cards will pile up in no time.

Store credit cards often have a higher interest rate and lure you in by sales and special deals when you sign on the dotted line. How many times have you been offered a 15% discount on a purchase in a department store if you would agree to put that purchase on a store credit card (that has 18% interest, or more)? The temptation of instant gratification is even present with that offer. You can have all the clothes you want *now*, but pay for them *later*. Many will pay much more for those clothes than they are worth by the time interest is paid on that purchase.

Burkett and Ramsey have been viewed as radicals to some, but they are the ones that understand how the pitfall of minimum payments undermine the effort of many Americans who are pursuing financial freedom. Proverbs 22:7 reminds us, "The rich rule over the poor, and the borrower is slave to the lender." If you cannot pay off your monthly statement balance, you are a slave to your credit cards.

The highest interest payment that many will ever pay is to credit card companies. Credits cards entrap you with convenience, the ability to make impulse purchases, and a low minimum payment. The result is classic and often repeated. Most people buy more than they can afford. Pay what you can now. Pay the rest later.

What could be wrong with that? The problem is that it will take you much longer than you planned to "pay later" and it will cost you much more than you wanted to pay.

PITFALL 4 - DOING IT ALONE

Have you ever met a know-it-all? A. J. Jacobs is a magazine editor who, in his mid-thirties, decided to read every page of the Encyclopedia Britannica. That's 32 volumes, 33,000 pages, and 44 million words. For one year and fifty-five days he read 100 pages per day. His accomplishment led to an appearance on *Who Wants To Be A Millionaire*. Unfortunately, all of his studying didn't help. Jacobs missed the $32,000 question that called for a definition of erythrocyte. Even though he had read every word of the "E" volume, he couldn't remember it meant "red blood cell." He walked away with $1,000 and ended up writing a book about his experience called, *The Know-It-All*.[26] He should have phoned a friend.

"The fear of the LORD is the beginning of knowledge; fools despise wisdom and instruction" (Proverbs 1:7). King Solomon, the wisest man to walk the earth, exhorted his sons to seek counsel when making decisions. Fortunately, millennials are doing better than previous generations when it comes to seeking advice.

> *"Asked about eight hypothetical situations – including receiving an inheritance, planning for retirement and buying a home – younger respondents in the survey were more likely on all counts to say they would look for professional advice. The biggest gap: buying a home, which 39% of millennials said they would seek help on, compared with only 9% of boomers. An inclination to seek help ahead of a big financial decision is a good thing."[27]*

[26]A. J. Jacobs, *The Know It All* (New York, NY: Simon & Schuster, 2005), 1-5.
[27]Kelly B. Grant, "Millennials Must Avoid the Pitfall of Going It Alone at All Costs," *CNBC* (Aug 2016).

Our dad always told us that, "A mentor is someone that has been where you have not been, they have done what you have not done, and they have seen what you have not seen. Much of your success in life will be determined by your relationships with these men and women."

Have you closed multiple million dollar deals, traveled the world, successfully ran a business, or given away a percentage of your income? Others have done all this and much, much more. Let's posture ourselves with greater humility and learn from so many that have gone before us. Without mentors our first attempts regularly end in failure or become much more difficult than they need to be because we do not know how to avoid common pitfalls. By positioning ourselves as learners we learn so much! You can too with the right approach. Who around you has handled their finances well? What can you learn from them?

CONNECT WITH
#MILLENNIALSANDMONEY

Pitfalls are scary. Especially when we keep falling in them. What pitfall did you read about that you have been falling into? What's the other road look like and how do you get down it?

CHAPTER SEVEN

READY, SET, GO!

WHAT ABOUT YOU?

What about you? What are your dreams? What are your goals? Where would you like to be in 10 years? What would you like to accomplish?

What is stopping you from beginning to pursue those dreams today? One of our favorite stories in the Bible is the story of David and Goliath. It is a great underdog story. A small, weak, untrained shepherd boy faces off with a huge, trained warrior named Goliath. Many know the result of the story: little David defeated Goliath in battle in spite of his diminutive size.

But did you know *why* David won the battle? David knew he would win the battle because he had prepared for the battle years prior to his encounter.

> *When the words that David spoke were heard, they repeated them before Saul, and he sent for him. And David said to Saul, "Let no man's heart fail because of him. Your servant will go and fight with this Philistine." And Saul said to David, "You are not able to go against this Philistine to fight with him, for you are but a youth, and he has been a man of war from his youth." But David said to Saul, "Your servant used to keep sheep for his father. And when there came a lion, or a bear, and took a lamb from the flock, I went after him and struck him and delivered it out of his mouth. And if he arose against me,*

I caught him by his beard and struck him and killed him. Your servant has struck down both lions and bears, and this uncircumcised Philistine shall be like one of them, for he has defied the armies of the living God." And David said, "The LORD who delivered me from the paw of the lion and from the paw of the bear will deliver me from the hand of this Philistine." And Saul said to David, "Go, and the LORD be with you!"[28]

Did you catch the reason for victory? "Your servant has struck down both lions and bears. This uncircumcised Philistine shall be like one of them" (dead). King Saul after hearing this young shepherd boy saw the conviction in his eyes and heard it in his voice he simply replied, "Go, and the Lord be with you!"

David wasn't a wimp, he wasn't untrained, he wasn't weak, and he certainly didn't get lucky. He had prepared for years for that battle and won as a result. You might be tempted to quit in the face of your financial Goliath. You may be paralyzed by your fears because you do not know where to begin.

There is no longer a need to feel that way. Now that you have completed *Millennials and Money*, you know where to begin. You have prepared to fight your financial Goliath. You do not have to fight this battle alone. Reach out to some potential mentors. Reach out to us through social media.

We have given you a game plan to win this battle. Just remember, if information was enough, we'd all be billionaires and have six pack abs. Thinking differently is a great place to start, but we also must change our actions if we expect our financial situation to improve. Our behavior has to change if we ever plan to experience financial freedom.

Like the rails of a train track, our beliefs and our behaviors have to be aligned in order to take us to our desired destination. Many of

[28] 1 Samuel 17:31-37 ESV

us ran foot races when we were children. The races usually looked the same. We would all line up at the start and someone would yell out these familiar words, "Ready, Set, Go." Some races we won, some we lost, and some we were just glad we finished. The three simple words "Ready, Set, Go" let us know it was time to act.

At the 1968 Olympics, an hour after the marathon's winner crossed the finish line, Tanzania's John Stephen Akhwari limped across the finish line, still injured from when he fell early in the race. Asked why he didn't quit, he said, "My country did not send me 7,000 miles to start this race. My country sent me to finish."

We are assuming you are reading *Millennials and Money* because you want to finish the financial race as winners. We want you to start well.

READY.

We both love comic strips. One of our favorites is *Dilbert*, one of the most popular comic strips ever created. The strip, authored by Scott Adams is published in 19 languages, 2,000 papers, in 57 countries. Adams, however, did not start out as a prolific writer. He credits much of his success to the advice of a lady he met in a class he was taking in order to become a certified, professional hypnotist.

This young lady told him to write down a specific goal fifteen times a day and to use his name in the sentence when he did. His sentence was, "Scott Adams will become a number one best-selling author." He began writing that goal long before he had ever written a book or even taken a writing course.[29]

If someone asked you to write down a specific financial goal, what would it be? What are you most passionate about? What do you want to do with this life you've been given?

Do you want to give away a million dollars to charity? Do you want to travel around the world? Do you want to reduce poverty in third world countries? Do you want to reduce illiteracy in your hometown? Do you want to start a foundation to help foster children find healthy, happy homes? Would you like to become a millionaire, start a business, raise a family, or become debt free? Would you like to be financially independent? What is it that you want to do with this life God has given you?

Maybe you think that setting the kinds of financial goals we are talking about in this book are way beyond your ability. Maybe being debt free and having the ability to give away as much as you want seems unattainable. It isn't. We love the African proverb, "How do you eat an elephant? One bite at a time." If you will commit yourself to small steps in the same direction for an extended period of time, you will be amazed at what you can accomplish.

SET.

Have you ever heard what many people called, "The Shortest Story Ever Written"? It was written by cancer survivor Portia Nelson. It has only five short chapters.

"The Shortest Story Ever Written"
Portia Nelson
CHAPTER 1
I walk down the street.
There is a deep hole in the sidewalk.
I fall in.
I am lost... I am helpless.
It isn't my fault.
It takes forever to find a way out.

CHAPTER 2

I walk down the same street.

There is a deep hole in the sidewalk.

I pretend I don't see it.

I fall in again.

I can't believe I am in the same place.

But, it isn't my fault.

It still takes me a long time to get out.

CHAPTER 3

I walk down the same street.

There is a deep hole in the sidewalk.

I see it is there.

I still fall in. It's a habit.

My eyes are open.

I know where I am.

It is my fault. I get out immediately.

CHAPTER 4

I walk down the same street.

There is a deep hole in the sidewalk.

I walk around it.

CHAPTER 5

I walk down another street.

When it comes to your finances, are you ready to walk down another street? The progression of this short story shows what a budget can do for you. A budget lets us know if we're going the wrong way, what holes we're falling into, and allows us to see when we need to go in a completely different direction. You will not reach your financial goals without a budget, which accomplishes goals for us: 1) It let's us see where we are. 2) It gives us a new direction to travel. 3) It helps us see the finish line.

The most important thing a budget does for us is to see how much money is left over after all our bills have been paid. These

---

[29]Tim Ferriss, *Tools of Titans* (Boston, MA: Houghton Mifflin Harcourt, 2016), 265.

are the dollars we have to find and put to work reducing debt, securing assets, or growing in interest bearing accounts.

One of our families' favorite childhood books is *Precious Present*. Our dad fell in love with this book instantly upon the discovery that his favorite college basketball coach read this book to his team every year on the first practice day.

The premise of *Precious Present* is a young boy conversing with an older man discussing a present that could make anyone happy forever. The boy was so excited with the thought of eternal happiness that he set his heart on one day receiving this precious present. He often wondered whether it would be a bicycle, a special ring, old gold coins buried by pirates, or simply just becoming happy.

He looked in the Wall Street Journal, on the top of mountains, the darkest caves, the dense and humid jungles, and below the sea, but never found the gift. The searching had taken its toll on the boy and he had begun to outgrow his youth. Eventually he stopped his search all together, and then it dawned on him. The precious present wasn't a gift. It was a moment in time: the PRESENT. Not the past or the future, but the right here, right now. He asked himself why he had missed this premise for so long and why he squandered so many precious moments looking for it when the truth was so simple.

Right now is the precious present and it is time to capitalize on it. Get to work on your budget today! Do it so you can locate the extra money you have to start your financial snowball.

Are you willing to move to a cheaper house, cut your cable, start a part-time job, reduce entertainment expenses, give up your morning coffee, fix meals at home, cut up your credit cards, switch to cash only, or cut any of a thousand other expenses? There will be some parts of your life that will have to change in order for you to reach your financial goals. These changes will be worth it in the long run. Before you can start (Go) you have to know how much you have to start *with*.

GO!

It is tempting to think that all successful people are just more educated, more talented, or more skilled in an area than we ever could be. Tim Ferris addresses that fallacy in *Tools of Titans*, "The superheroes you have in your mind (idols, icons, titans, billionaires, etc.) are all nearly walking flaws who've maximized 1 or 2 strengths. "Malcom Gladwell, journalist, speaker, and author, observed that, 'In fact, researches have settled on what they believe is the magic number for true expertise: ten thousand hours.'" That's right, average, flawed, common, imperfect people just like you and me can succeed simply by repeating the best practices that lead to preferred futures. W.H. Auden adds, "Routine, in an intelligent man is a sign of ambition." Paying off 100% of your debt is the preferred future and our budget is the routine that will get you there.[30]

YOU CAN SUCCEED SIMPLY BY REPEATING THE BEST PRACTICES THAT LEAD TO PREFERRED FUTURES.

Calvin Coolidge said, "Nothing in the world can take the place of persistence. Talent will not; nothing is more common than unsuccessful men with talent. Genius will not; unrewarded genius is almost a proverb. Education will not; the world is full of educated derelicts. Persistence and determination alone are omnipotent. The slogan 'press on' has solved, and always will solve the problems of the human race." In chapter one, we warned

---

[30]Tim Ferriss, Tools of Titans (Boston: Houghton Mifflin Harcourt, 2016), 23.

you that gaining financial freedom wasn't going to be easy. It takes persistence and determination. Whoever loves discipline loves knowledge (Proverbs 12:1).

The worst kind of investment in the world is an investment that depreciates quickly (loses value). Worse than depreciation is paying interest on depreciation. That is what we are doing when we carry most debt. It is also why we must avoid debt at all costs.

Debt is our enemy. It introduces itself as an innocent friend that wants to help us get what we want most in life. Once we begin using it, the hooks are set. We pay more for every item we purchase, we pay longer for every item than we should, and we become enslaved.

Debt is a harsh taskmaster, driving us to work because we have to pay the bills. Throw off your shackles; eradicate your debt! Commit to not adding new debts of any type as you journey through the process we have described in this book.

KNOW YOUR ENEMY.

List out all of your debt balances least to greatest, it's time for war.

DEBT	AMOUNT OWED	INTEREST RATE

Consider again the Smiths whom utilized the debt eliminator in Chapter 2. One of the reasons it's important to see the numbers on these examples (like debt eliminator, investment calculator) is because it is really difficult to see how unescapable the results really are. The overwhelming evidence is so strong that it can't be argued or debated. Unfortunately, most millennials are never taught these basic financial concepts in high school or college level classes.

State your commitment to avoid new debts and sign your name.

i.e. I will not go into any new debt while I'm at war with my existing balances.

_____   _____
SIGNATURE   DATE

CONNECT WITH US.

We want to see you win, we want to see you beat your debts, and we want to see you pass the finish line of financial independence. Gaining financial independence as we've discussed doesn't happen overnight. It is the result of hard work, dedication, lots of prayers, and consistent small wins.

Fortunately for us, as a generation, we have the world's greatest mentors and coaches who have put their wisdom into print for us. There really is no excuse. The best athletes in the world have coaches and the best businessmen and women have consultants and mentors. Do not feel like you have to go on this journey alone.

CONNECT WITH
#MILLENNIALSANDMONEY

Do not feel like you have to go on this journey alone.
Connect with us via social media so we can be a source of
encouragement to you along your journey.

READY.

Write your name and the goal you want to achieve.

_____

_____

SET.

1. Complete your budget.
2. How much money do I have at the end of my bills? $ _____
3. What expenses am I willing to cut?

_____   _____

_____   _____

4. How can I generate additional monthly income?

_____

_____

GO.

Write your debts into a debt eliminator worksheet.

DEBT	AMOUNT OWED	INTEREST RATE

ABOUT THE AUTHORS

As mentioned in the dedication, Sara and William have been greatly influenced by their parents, Steve and Tina Wright. Growing up in the same home, Sara and William have been taught the importance of good financial decisions and making every penny count. They were excited to write this book together, with the help of their family, to impart the financial wisdom they have learned.

SARA MEADOWS

Sara is passionate about working with children, going on missions trips, reading, traveling, and spending time with her husband.

Sara and her husband, Ethan, live in Apex, NC. Sara is a graduate of Campbell University and a real estate agent with Fonville Morisey in the Raleigh/Apex area.

WILLIAM WRIGHT

William loves the outdoors, researching, and reading. When William isn't researching, he can be found hunting, snowboarding, golfing or fishing.

William and his wife Rebecca reside in West Palm Beach, FL. William is the Founder and CEO of Digital Rocket. Digital Rocket specializes in Search Engine Optimization, Website Development and Digital Marketing.
Visit www.digitalrocket.church for more information.

Made in the USA
Columbia, SC
20 August 2024

40739249R00049